How Do Engineers Solve Problems?

HOUGHTON MIFFLIN HARCOURT

PHOTOGRAPHY CREDITS: COVER ©Digital Vision/Getty Images; 3 (bl) ©Hans Peter Merten/Getty Images; 3 (br) ©D. Hurst/Alamy Images; 4 (b) ©Blue Jean Images/Alamy Images; 5 (br) ©Wealan Pollard/Alamy Images; 6 (br) ©Radius Images/Alamy Images; 7 (t) ©Image Source/Getty Images; 8 (b) ©GerryRousseau/Alamy Images; 9 (b) ©Sami Sarkis/Getty Images; 11 (br) ©Elena Elisseeva/Alamy Images

Printed in Mexico

ISBN: 978-0-544-07249-7

9 10 11 12 0908 20 19 18 17 16

4500607981   A B C D E F G

Look at these words.

technology	engineer
environment	design process

Look for answers to these questions.

What is technology?

What technology do children use to get to school?

What classroom technology do you use?

How does technology affect our environment?

What do engineers do?

What is the design process?

How can the design process help you solve a problem?

What is technology?

Technology is what we make to meet our needs and solve our problems. Technology is all around us!

Cars get us from place to place. Long ago, people used their hands to make cars. Today, people have help. They use robots.

Telephones let us talk to people who are far away. Washing machines help us wash clothes. Ovens help us cook food. What other technology do you use?

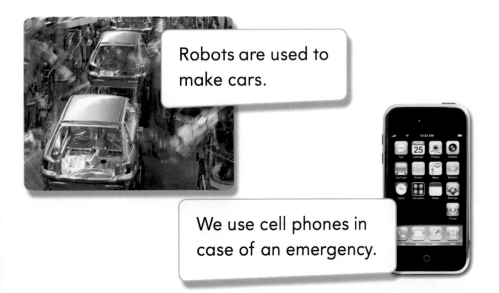

Robots are used to make cars.

We use cell phones in case of an emergency.

What technology do children use to get to school?

Some children go to school in cars. Others ride bikes. Both cars and bikes are technology.

A car's engine makes it move. The wheel turns the car. The brake makes the car stop. Seat belts keep people safe.

Think about how your bike moves. You use your feet to make it move. Bike handles help you turn left or right. You wear a helmet. It keeps your head safe.

A seat belt is important technology for safety.

What classroom technology do you use?

A computer is a kind of technology. You can find out more about animals using a computer and the Internet. You can use a computer to write a report, too!

A whiteboard helps you learn in different ways. You can write words or draw pictures on a whiteboard.

A pencil helps you write. Scissors help you cut paper. A thumbtack holds up your artwork.

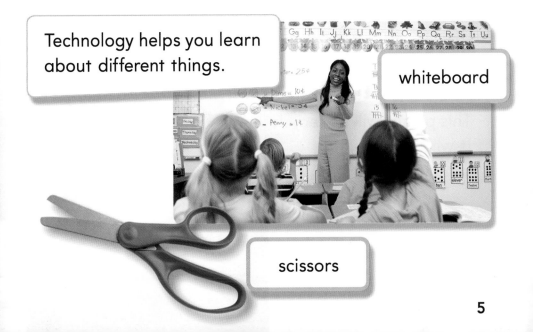

Technology helps you learn about different things.

whiteboard

scissors

How does technology affect our environment?

The environment is all the living and nonliving things in a place. Living things are plants, animals, and people. Nonliving things include the technology we use.

Sometimes, technology can harm, or hurt, the environment. Using too much plastic is not good. It fills the environment with trash. To help the environment, you can recycle plastic bottles. They can be turned into something new. Or, you can reuse a plastic cup. Wash it and use it again.

This plastic will be recycled. It will be made into something new.

Some engineers make plans for buildings.

What do engineers do?

An engineer is a scientist. An engineer uses math and science. Engineers help people and solve problems.

Engineers also make plans. A plan shows how to make something. Some engineers build trains and ships.

Engineers also design computer programs.

What is the design process?

The design process is a set of steps that engineers follow to solve problems.

1. Find a Problem
2. Plan and Build
3. Test and Improve
4. Redesign
5. Communicate

One problem is that people often walk in flower gardens. What is something you can build to protect the flowers? How can you test and improve your design?

This sign might help to solve the problem.

You can keep a record of your design process. Write ideas in a notebook. Use a computer to organize your work. Some people use a recorder to record their ideas. Then they listen to their ideas later. A video camera is a helpful tool, too. It records moving pictures of your work.

Sharing your design is important. You can write about it. Or, you can tell others about it.

A computer can help you organize and share your design.

How can the design process help you solve a problem?

You can solve a problem by following these steps.

1. Find a Problem

   Your class paints pictures. The pictures stick together when you stack them.

2. Plan and Build

   You plan to hang the pictures from a clothesline. You build a clothesline.

3. Test and Improve

   Paint drips to the floor when you hang the pictures from the clothesline. You improve the design by using two clotheslines.

A painting takes time to dry.

4. Redesign

You clip each picture at the top and bottom. You make sure that the pictures face the ceiling. Now the paint does not drip.

5. Communicate

You tell other children about your new design.

One clothesline is not enough. The paint drips on the floor.

Make a List

Work with a partner. Act out using a kind of technology that is in your classroom. Have your partner guess the technology. Switch roles. Then make a list of each kind of technology. Next to each item, write how it solves a problem.

Research and Write

Use books or the Internet to research jobs that engineers do. Choose your favorite job, and make a poster. Draw a picture of an engineer doing the job. Write about what the engineer does to solve a problem.